Eureka!

Challenging **Maths** and **Numerical Reasoning** Exam Questions for **11+** Exam Preparation

The Eureka! 11+ Confidence series

CEM-style Practice Exam Papers covering:
Comprehension, Verbal Reasoning,
Non-Verbal Reasoning and Numerical Reasoning

Numerical Reasoning: Advanced Training Workbooks

Tough exam paper questions and detailed explanations of
how to tackle them, to increase speed and reduce error.

Verbal Reasoning: Advanced Training Workbooks

The 1000-Word Brain Boost is an intensive course teaching
Synonyms, Antonyms, Odd-One-Out, Analogy,
Vocabulary and Cloze, in CEM-style exam paper questions.
The answer section explains the important subtleties and
distintions that many 11+ candidates find challenging.

ISBN-10: 1512096385
ISBN-13: 978-1512096385

First Published in the United Kingdom in 2015 by Eureka! Eleven Plus Exams.
Revision dated 3 August 2015

Eureka! Eleven Plus Exams is grateful to Sian Williams and Leona Bourne.

Please check **www.eureka11plus.org/updates** for any updates or clarifications for this book.
Tutors seeking volume discounts are advised to contact the office email address below.

We are all human and vulnerable to error. Eureka! Eleven Plus Exams is very grateful to any reader who notifies us of any unnoticed error, so we can immediately correct it and provide a tangible reward.

Preparing for 11+ with this book

Pupils approaching the 11+ Examination face many challenges, including lack of time, uncertainty over what is required, and an ever-changing and secretive testing environment.

Plain "mathematics" questions are progressively being replaced with more demanding "numerical reasoning" questions. Selective schools are increasingly interested in not only rote recall of methods but also the ability to understand questions expressed in prose and skilfully apply (sometimes several) mathematical principles to arrive at an answer.

The *Eureka! 11+ Challenging Maths and Numerical Reasoning* series of books to provide focused preparation for pupils and their busy parents. Questions are expressed in words, with the pupils learning the habit of extracting the relevant numbers and key facts. Most questions are multi-part, reflecting the trend in examinations to challenge pupils skills at progressively higher levels as the question unfolds.

These questions are the upper echelon of what is tested at 11+. Although they need only Key Stage 2 concepts, they are challenging because they require good command of multiple skills simultaneously. Pupils, and perhaps even parents, will find very few of these questions to be very easy. Thankfully, the real exam will contain many easier questions, but preparation time is best spent on those which present greater challenges and therefore more learning opportunities.

When answering the questions
- Set yourself a target, e.g. "3 questions in half an hour"
- Underline the key information if the question is lengthy
- Write your working clearly *and in full* so you can check easily

Go through the answers **soon** after doing the questions
- Do not be sad if you have made mistakes: learn from them
- Many questions cover areas where even strong pupils are prone to errors
- Watch out for the Traps described
- Incorporate the Tips into your methods in future
- See if the Method suggested is quicker or less open to error than yours

For any examination, diligent practice, carefully analysing errors, mulling over methods, and developing and testing your own preferred approaches pay enormous dividends.

Ainu has built a traditional cone-shaped teepee for her school carnival, adorning it with a large flag, grey on one side and black on the other.

The flagpole rests exactly on the sloping north wall of the teepee and extends beyond it in a straight line. The flag hangs vertically from the whole upper half of the flagpole. It has a triangular shape, starting at its narrowest, as a point at the apex of the teepee, and gradually becoming taller so that it hangs down to meet the teepee wall. At the top end of the flagpole the flag hangs all the way to the ground, touching the south perimeter of the base of the teepee.

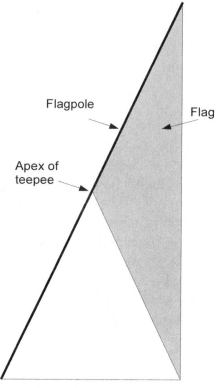

A celebratory bead garland 8·8 m long that has been made to fit exactly to the circular base of the teepee. The apex of the teepee is 3 m above the ground.

During this celebration, please respect the tradition amongst Ainu's ancestors that π should be taken as 22/7.

What is the area of the grey side of the flag?

Answer: _____ m².

62

Robotron is training robots to be released to travel the world to help children with their maths homework. Unfortunately the robots have only a simple program to guide their movements.

Step 1   If possible, move forward one square and return to step 1; otherwise go to step 2.

Step 2   Turn right 90 degrees. Return to step 1.

Moving forward one square takes 1 minute, but turning takes no time at all.
The 4 robots, Artoo, Beetu, Sittoo and Ditu embark on the task, starting from different positions. Each robot may either successfully exit from the maze, or get stuck travelling round a circuit inside the maze.

(i) For each robot, indicate the exit number by which it leaves the maze, or write "stuck" if the robot does not exit.

Artoo   Exit number _____

Beetu   Exit number _____

Sittoo   Exit number _____

Ditu   Exit number _____

(ii) Choose one robot who gets stuck: Name of a robot chosen: _____

In the circuit in which this robot is trapped, how much time does it take from one occasion the robot passes through a point on the circuit, to the next occasion he passes through that point travelling in the same direction?

Answer: Time interval = _____ minutes

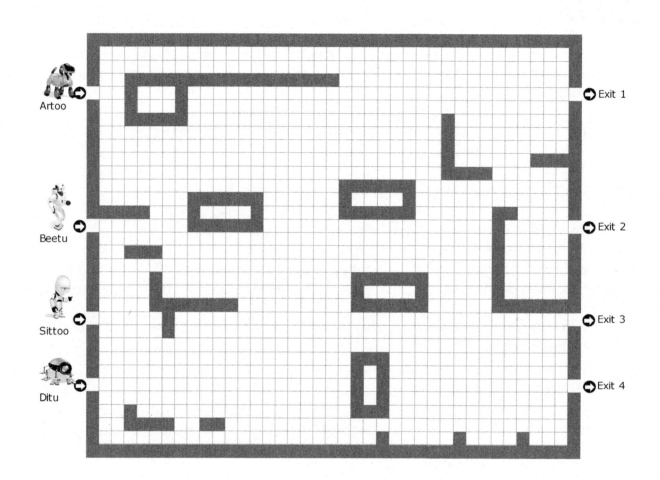

Artoo

Beetu

Sittoo

Ditu

Exit 1

Exit 2

Exit 3

Exit 4

Flavius the stonemason and his team had completed the elaborate sculptures of the Roman emperor's 20 victories over the barbarians.

However, the emperor now demanded a giant set of stone numbers, from I to XX, to stand alongside the sculptures.

One stonemason takes 8 hours to chisel the Roman symbol "I". Two stonemasons would take 4 hours, and 4 would take 2 hours, and so on.

One stonemason takes 12 hours to chisel a "V" symbol, and 16 hours for an "X" symbol.

There are 8 stonemasons on the team. If they all work together, how many hours will the team take to chisel the stone numbers?

Time taken = _____ hours

64

Imagine a new shorthand symbol, ►, is introduced. It is defined as the sum of the whole numbers between (and including) two numbers. For example, 11 ► 14 = 11 + 12 + 13 + 14 = 50.

(i)   What is 1 ► 10 ?   Answer _____

(ii)   What is 1 ► 11 ?   Answer _____

(iii)   What is 1 ► 12?   Answer _____

(iv)   What is 1 ► 13?   Answer _____

Examine the pattern.

(v)   What is (1 ► 200) – (1 ► 199) ?   Answer _____

(vi)   What is (1000 ► 2000) – (1001 ► 1999) ?   Answer _____

Extend the principle you have observed.
If a and b are whole numbers, and a < b:

(vii)   What is (a ► b) – ((a+1) ► b)?

                          Answer _____

(viii)   Provide a simplified expression for (1 ► a) + ((a+1) ► b). Your answer should include the ► symbol.

                          Answer _____

65

"Think of a number between 100 and 999 with digits in decreasing order," quipped Quentin. His long-suffering sister Marjorie complied.
"Now make a new number by reversing the order of the digits."
Marjorie nodded.
"Calculate the first number minus the second number. What is the last digit of your answer?"
"Six," replied Marjorie.
"Then the full answer to your subtraction is 496," beamed Quentin triumphantly. He ran off laughing. Marjorie resolved to find out how this trick worked.

(i) If Marjorie's first number had instead been 321, what would the result of her subtraction have been?

Answer   _____

(ii) If Marjorie's first number had been 832, what would the result of her subtraction have been?

Answer   _____

(iii) Explain why the middle digit of the subtraction result always turns out to be 9.

Answer   _____

          _____

(iv) Is there a relationship between the first and last digit of the subtraction result? Why?

Answer   _____

          _____

          _____

66

Marina designs a unique fish tank, shown below.

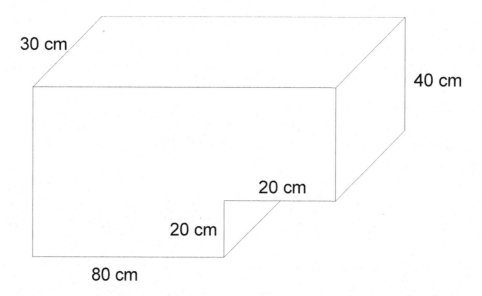

(i) What is the total area of all the external surfaces of the **vertical** glass walls. (Do not count top face of the tank or the floors of the tank. Do not count the inside surfaces of the walls of the tank.)

Answer _____ cm²

(iii) Marina fills the tank using a hose providing 100 ml per second. If she starts filling it at 14:00, at what time does the tank become full?

Answer _____:_____

67

Thomas throws a 12-sided die, with faces numbered from 1 to 12. What, as a fraction in its lowest terms, is the probability of throwing:

(i) An even number? _____

(ii) A number smaller than 5? _____

(iii) A multiple of 3? _____

(iv) A number more than 10? _____

(v) A number that isn't 6? _____

(vi) A number that does not contain the digit "1"? _____

Ursula arrives with a pair of standard dice, each of which has faces numbered 1 to 6.
They play a game in which Thomas throws his die and reads his score, and at the same time Ursula throws her pair of dice and reads her score as the sum of the scores of the two dice.

(vii) The maximum Thomas can score is 12. What is the maximum Ursula can score? _____

(viii) What is the probability that Thomas scores 12? _____

(ix) What is the probability that Ursula scores 12? _____

(x) Who has the greater probability of scoring 12? _____

68

Otto has an 8-sided die, whose faces are numbered from 1 to 8.

He throws it three times and writes down the 3 individual scores in the order that they were thrown to make a 3-digit number, which he calls "x". For example, if he throws first 5, then 6, then 3, his value of x is 563.

Indicate for each of the following statements, whether it is certain, likely, unlikely or impossible. Underline the appropriate word.

(i) x is 319.

Certain   Likely   Unlikely   Impossible

(ii) x is greater than 120.

Certain   Likely   Unlikely   Impossible

(iii) 4x + 8 is an even number.

Certain   Likely   Unlikely   Impossible

(iv) 2x < 250.

Certain   Likely   Unlikely   Impossible

(v) No digit of x is less than 7.

Certain   Likely   Unlikely   Impossible

69

Five pupils are discussing their test results. Roberto's score, 75, is 5 above the group's mean. Philomena scored 6 more than the mode. The only pair to obtain the same score were Kelvin and Calvin, who shared the lowest position with scores of 63.

(i) What was the mode score? _____

(ii) What was the median score? _____

(iii) What was the range? _____ (this should be one number)

(iv) Abigail was the fifth pupil.
What was her score? _____

Myrtle joins the group. Including Myrtle, the mean is now 68.

(v) What is Myrtle's score? _____

(vi) What is the median now? _____

The number of trees remaining in the Magic Forest Kingdom has been falling.

Fairy Year	Oak	Elm
370	65	80
371	60	70
373	50	50
374	45	40

(i) Draw these data on the axes below. Cover dates from Fairy Year 370 to 380.

Use the graph to project future counts assuming the rate of reduction continues in the same manner.

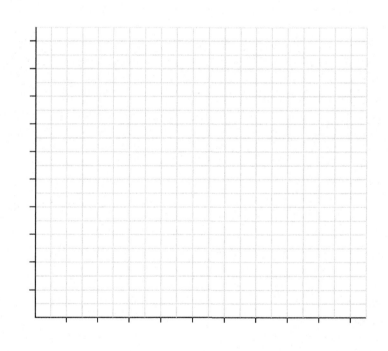

(ii) In what year will the number of oaks fall to 20?

_____

(iii) In what year will the number of elms fall to 0?

Answer: Year   _____

Year 372 had no tree census.

(iv) Estimate from the graph the likely number of oak in 372.   _____

(v) Estimate from the graph the likely number of elm in 372.   _____

71

General Zargaz reported to the Emperor that the survey of the Imperial island of Bulbulia had been completed (as shown below). He announced the key statistics.

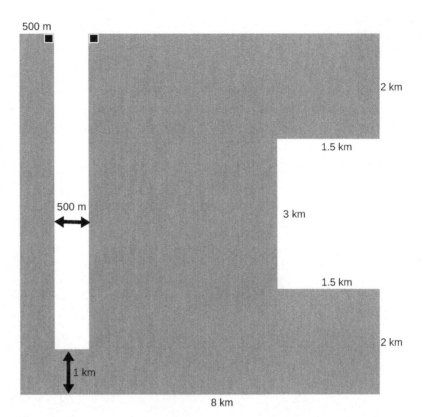

(i) What was the perimeter, in km?

_____ km

(ii) What was the area, in km²?

_____ km²

"Your majesty, we could increase Bulbulia's security by building a wall between the bell towers, marked on this map as 2 black squares, and then filling in with rubble the area of sea thus enclosed. Amazingly, the Imperial mathematician says this will increase the land area of the island while reducing the perimeter!"

(iii) In square metres, by how much will the land area increase? _____ m²

(iv) In metres, by how much will the perimeter be reduced? _____ m.

72

Mr Dudah is determined to save money in building his new racetrack after losing his previous racetrack through an ill-considered bet. The expensive, highly reflective paint used for the arrows to guide sports-people around the track is a prime target for cost reduction.

The new track has the same perimeter, 1 km, as the old track. The old track has arrows of the design shown as A below. The new track will use the design shown as B below.

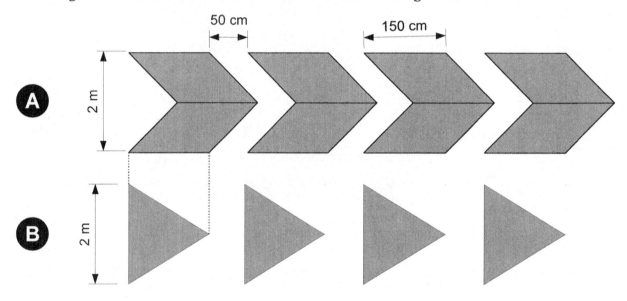

(i) By what percentage will Mr Dudah reduce his expenditure on this paint if he uses design B for the new Camptown Race Track?

Percentage reduction = _____ %

(ii) At £80 per m², what will the total cost of painting design B on the perimeter of the race track?

Cost = £ _____

Einat's research project took her to the Arctic Ocean, surveying polar bear habitats. When her friend Marie emailed her complaining that the temperature in Swansea was chilly at 5°C, Einat pointed out that the temperature on the boat was currently 20 degrees lower. Moreover the day before it had been 12 degrees below even that.

Marie sympathised with her friend suffering for the sake of science, and asked if these current temperatures were unusual. Marie replied with a Table of the daily temperatures at noon for two recent weeks.

	M	T	W	T	F	S	S
Week 1	-15	-12	-5	1	3	2	-8
Week 2	1	-1	7	0	-3	6	-5

(i) What was the temperature yesterday?

Answer _____ °C.

(ii) Was it unusual in comparison with those occurring in the 2 weeks of measurements shown? In what way?

Answer _____

_____

_____

(iii) In the 2 weeks of measurements, what was the median?

Answer _____ °C.

74

Travelling to support his favourite darts team, Roland departed London on Tuesday via Heathrow Airport. As the plane lifted off, he glanced at his watch, which read 09:30. As it touched down in Tokyo, Japan, the pilot announced that it was Wednesday, and that the local time was 06:30. Roland had spent the entire flight listening to a repeating play-list consisting of 24 five-minute tunes on his portable music player.

He remembered that when he had recently telephoned his friend in Tokyo, 1300 London time had corresponded to 2200 Tokyo time.

(i) Based on his recollection of the telephone call, what is the time difference between London and Tokyo?

Answer _____ hours

(ii) At the time he landed in Tokyo, what time was it in London?

Answer _____

(iii) How much time had the flight taken?

Answer _____ hours

(iv) On average, how fast had the plane been flying over the 6000 mile trip, in miles per hour?

Answer _____ miles per hour

(iv) How many times had he heard his play-list of tunes during the flight?

Answer _____

Kinder than his fairytale counterpart, the giant who had caught you creeping into his castle offers you an alternative to being eaten.

(i) "Tell me the amount of wood, in cubic metres, in my new table!" It is sketched below.

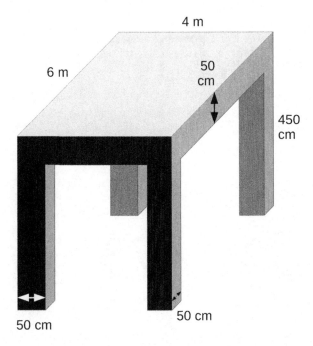

4 m

6 m

50 cm

450 cm

50 cm

50 cm

Volume of wood in table _____ m³

(ii) "Tell me the total surface area of the 5 outwardly directed visible surfaces!"
He means the top surface and the 4 faces shaped like the inverted U shown in black in the diagram.

Area of the five faces _____ m²

Fill the missing digits into the ☐ symbols.

(i) $518 - 3\,\square\,2 = 19\,\square$

(ii) $98\,\square - \square\,\square\,2 = 473$

(iii) $2\,\square\,3 \times \square = \square\,\square\,17$

Wallace was given a large black disc made of cardboard. He carefully cut out two equilateral triangles, touching corner to corner and touching the circle at their other corners. He made the triangles as large as he could possibly could, given the size of the cardboard disc. Each side was 14 cm.

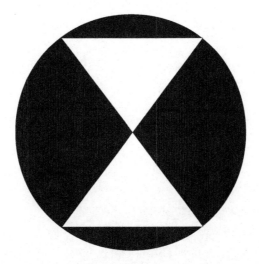

(i) What was the total of the perimeters of the two triangles he cut out?

Answer _____ cm

(ii) What was the area of the disc, before he started cutting? Take π to be 22/7.

Answer _____ cm².

(iii) He receives a fresh disk of the same size as before. What is the largest number of such triangles he can cut from this disc?

Answer _____ cm².

78

Obsessive Cecily likes to measure and count. The school pond is a long, thin rectangle 1·57 m by 10 m. A corner of the pond is shown in the figure below.

On it Cecily has counted 50 water lilies.

She cannot resist measuring them. Each is a disc with diameter 20 cm.

It rains that day. Some of the raindrops fall onto the water lilies, whereas the others fall directly into the pond water.

What proportion of raindrops fall onto the water lilies?

(Take π to be 3·14.)

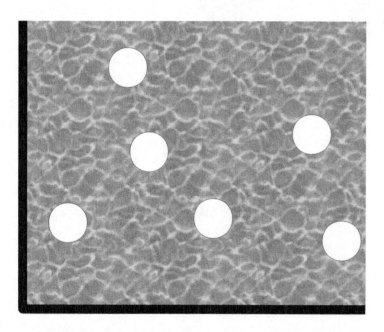

Answer _____

79

(i) Mrs Frownsome announced to the class that the homework was questions 18 to 57 inclusive. The pupils sighed but only Gabrielle found the courage to speak up.

"Please Miss, can we have a bit less?"

"Less? Less? Outrageous!"

The pupils put on their most pleading faces.

"Alright, you can start at at 23 and finish at 52."

What percentage reduction in the number of questions had she given?

Answer: _____%

(ii) Gabrielle found it much easier to get through pages in her science fiction novel, whizzing through at 2 pages a minute.

She started this evening at the beginning of page 60. Exactly 15 minutes later, which page had she just finished reading?

Answer: Page _____

80

Harry and Ron have some apple, orange and pear slices.

Harry has 5 more orange slices than Ron. Ron has 3 more pear slices than Harry. Harry has two apple slices and Ron has twice as many. Ron has the same number of apple slices as he has orange slices. Harry has as many orange slices as Ron has Pear slices.

(i)   How many fruit slices do they have altogether?

        Answer   _____

(ii)   How many pear slices are there altogether?

        Answer   _____

(iii)   What is the difference between Harry's total number of slices
        and Ron's total number of slices?

        Answer   _____

81

"It's all very well having gained freedom from tyranny," moaned Tiffany, "but now our overlords have been expelled, we have to do everything ourselves. I've been trudging round for ages weeding the grass perimeter of Liberty Square."

Gordon accepted that Tiffany had indeed weeded 480 metres of pathway on her own, but countered, "Just spare a thought for me! I will shortly start to hose down the entire concrete area of the square, with a few helpers. We each can do one square metre per minute. Imagine how long this is going to take us?"

What Gordon hadn't mentioned was the number of helpers that were joining him: 19.

(i) How long will the task take?

            Answer   _____ minutes

(ii) If Tiffany had that team with her instead, how long would they take to do the weeding? Each person can weed 1 metre per minute.

            Answer   _____ minutes

(iii) How much more time did Tiffany have to spend, **in hours and minutes**, because she was doing the work on her own?

            Answer   _____ hours _____ minutes

82

In the giant Discount Devastation sale, everything in the shop was on discount.

(i) Delighted shoppers were only paying £21 for designer sunglasses after the 30% discount. What was the pre-sale price of the sunglasses?

Answer   £ _____

(ii) Sylvester wants to purchase 2 shirts with the £40 he has. Unfortunately the pre-sale price of the shirts is £25 each. What percentage discount must he obtain in order to be able to buy them?

Percentage discount needed = _____

(ii)
"I'm so sorry," the assistant said when Ivan presented his card to pay for his trousers. "You will indeed get 30% off the pre-sale price of £40, but we have to charge 5% extra for payments using this Zanzibar Express card, because the Zanzibar Corporation charges us so much to process the payment."

How much will Ivan pay for the trousers?

Answer   £ _____

83

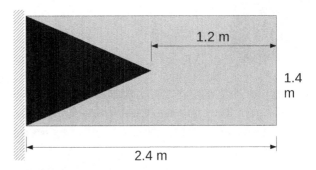

(i) His Excellency the Grand Poo Bah of Pantaloon was displeased at the flag of his country displayed at the United Nations. Staring closely at the black triangle, he demanded to know what percentage of the flag area it represented.

What did the flagmaster-general reply?   _____ %

(ii) "Aha! I *thought* there was something funny about it. Our declaration of independence states clearly that the black area should be exactly *one third* of the grey area. Why have you not done this correctly?"

What did the flagmaster-general reply?   _____

(iii) Only after Pantaloon's representative had left would the President of Residuum enter the flagmaster-general's office, so deep was the animosity between the two leaders.

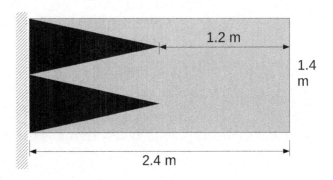

"Ridding ourselves of those ghastly Pantaloons took us two huge and glorious wars, each costing us the lives of one eighth of our population. Our flag has two triangles to represent this, each one-eighth of the overall flag area. On this flag you have made, the triangles look too small. I demand you check and correct this!"

What percentage of the total flag area will the flagmaster-general have to change from grey to black to satisfy him?

Answer   _____ %

84

At the fair, Uri is given a choice of 6 barrels. He must choose one barrel, reach into it, and draw out one of the identical-looking parcels within it. Some of the parcels contain a radio-controlled helicopter, others contain a video game, and all the others contain rusty springs.

The organisers announce that they filled the barrels with gifts in the numbers shown below:

Barrel	I	II	III	IV	V	VI
Helicopter	2	1	4	3	5	6
Video game	2	3	2	1	2	8
Springs	3	4	2	1	3	10

(i) He really wants a helicopter. Which barrel should he choose? _____

(iii) If, instead, he wants a video game, which barrel should he choose? _____

(ii) What, as a fraction in its lowest terms, is the chance of him getting a video game if he chooses box VI?

_____

(iv) Horrible Henry steals the barrels, but as he runs away, he trips over and drops barrels II and VI, which he then leaves behind. In its lowest terms, what fraction of the helicopters has he escaped with?

_____

85

The sweat may have been trickling from his brow, but Ferdinand's days of chiselling had been well rewarded. The giant wooden question mark stood gleaming in the afternoon sun. Even the fine metal sheet used to attach the upper section to the lower, "dot", section, had fitted perfectly.

(i) What was the volume of wood in the whole question mark?

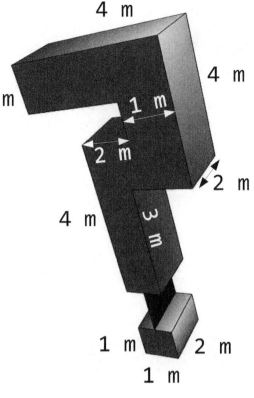

Answer _____ m³.

His wife, Imelda, had asked for the upper section to be painted: the front surface were to be blue and the equal-sized back surface to be red; all other wooden surfaces were to be painted white. (The fine metal sheet and lower section would be left alone). All wooden edges of the upper section were to be painted with a patriotic yellow stripe.

(ii) What area was to be painted blue?

Answer _____ m².

(iii) What area was to be painted white?

Answer _____ m².

(iv) What was the total length of yellow stripe?

Answer _____ m.

The pitter-patter of tiny feet filled the kitchen as Percival, Qasim and Rollo hopped on and off the kilogram weighing scales. "When the two of you are on this thing," mewed Rollo, "it says 9. But when Qasim and I are on it, it says 11."
"That's nothing!" retorted Qasim. "With you two on it, it reads 14."
The noise alerted Susan who shooed them away.

How much did each cat weigh?

Percival _____ kg

Qasim _____ kg

Rollo _____ kg

"Something is not right," mused Susan, staring at the display screen. With nothing on the scales, the readout was 1 kg. Knowing that the scales are over-reading by 1kg, what do you now think each cat weighed?

Percival _____ kg

Qasim _____ kg

Rollo _____ kg

Curling up and disappearing into the morning sunshine, Rosalind's staircase is a masterpiece of engineering. Each stair is a wooden slat, at an angle 36 degrees different from each of its neighbours. Each stair is 20 cm higher than the one below. (There is a stair level with the floor level of each floor.)

The staircase connects the floors of the new Tower 51 building, which has a ground floor and 51 further floors numbered 1 to 51. The floors are 3 metres apart.

(i) Frank walks from floor 20 to floor 21, walking on every stair on the way. How many stairs does he walk on?

Answer _____

(ii) On the staircase, he passes James, who is walking down from the floor 51 to the cafeteria on floor 1 in a similarly methodical manner. How many stairs does James step on?

Answer _____

(iii) "I'm dizzy," complained James on reaching floor 1. Through how many complete circles had he turned during his descent?

Answer _____

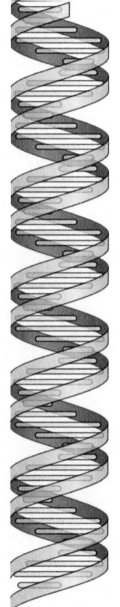

88

"Next year I will be twice as old as both of you put together," announced Colin.

"Well, I am four years older than Charlie," responded Cerys.

"Cerys, I am already 3 times as old as you will be next year," retorted Colin.

(i) How old is Charlie?

Answer _____ years

(ii) If it is 1990 now, in what year will Colin be twice as old as Charlie?

Answer _____

89

(i) On this graph, draw the triangle with vertices at:
D (-3,1),
E (-1, 5·5) and
F (1,1).

(ii) Draw its reflection in the diagonal line.

(iii) The rectangle PQRS has its bottom left corner, S, at (-8, -10). Its top left corner, P, is 12 units above that point. Its area is 18. Draw PQRS.

(iv) Draw the reflection of PQRS in the diagonal line.

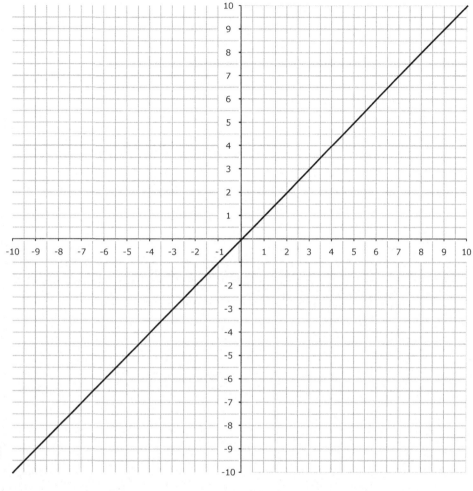

(v) PQRS and its reflection have a region of overlap. What is the area of this overlap? Express this as a fraction in its lowest terms.

Answer _____

90

(i) St Olaf's school has 90 pupils. For every 10 girls there are only 8 boys.

How many more girls than boys does the school have?

Answer _____

(ii) There is one spectacle-wearing pupil for every 2 pupils who do not wear spectacles. How many pupils wear spectacles?

Answer _____

(iii) The number of pupils who cannot sing is one eighth the number who can. How many can sing?

Answer _____

Answer 61

Area = **4·2 m²**.

Method. The garland's circumference, 8·8 m, is 2 π r. Its radius, r, is therefore 8·8 / (2× 22/7)
= 8·8/2/22×7
=   4·4/22×7
=   0·2 ×7
=   1·4

Because the far end of the flag hangs directly down to the ground, and the flagpole continues in the direction of the tent surface, the wide edge of the flag must be twice the height of the tent apex.

Area of triangle tip

To calculate the area of the flag, remember that the formula (½) base × height can be applied using *any of the three sides of a triangle as the "base"*. Just remember that the height must be measured perpendicularly to the base.

Area of triangle
= ½ base × height
= ½ 6 × 1·4
= **4·2 m²**.

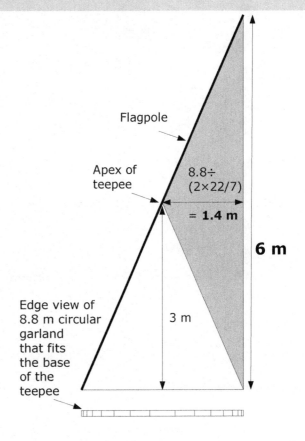

Flagpole

Apex of
teepee

8.8÷
(2×22/7)

= 1.4 m

6 m

3 m

Edge view of
8.8 m circular
garland
that fits
the base
of the
teepee

Answer 62

(i) Exits:

Artoo: **Stuck**

Beetu: **Exit 3**

Sittoo: **Exit 2**

Ditu: **Exit 1**

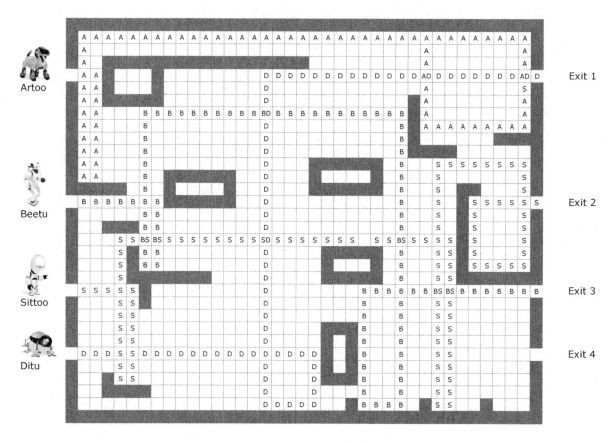

(ii) Only **Artoo** gets stuck.

When counting the squares in the circuit, make sure to count each square only once.
Number of squares in circuit = 30.
Time interval = **30 minutes.**

Answer 63

Method

In general, tabulate the digits in groups. Use any symmetries that are helpful.

Number range	Number	Digits used "I"	"V"	"X"
One to ten				
	I	1		
	II	2		
	III	3		
	IV	1	1	
	V		1	
	VI	1	1	
	VII	2	1	
	VIII	3	1	
	IX	1		1
	X			1
Total		**14**	**5**	**2**

Eleven to twenty are the same, but with an "X" at the beginning of each number, which you can use as a short-cut:

Eleven to twenty				
First digit				10
Second digit		14	5	2
Total		**14**	**5**	**12**
Grand total		**28**	**10**	**14**

Time taken if one stonemason is doing the work

$$= 28 \times 8 + 10 \times 12 + 14 \times 16$$
$$= 224 \quad + 120 \quad + 224$$
$$= 568 \text{ hours}$$

Time taken by a team of 8 stonemasons

$$= 568 \div 8$$
$$= \textbf{71 hours.}$$

Answer **64**

Handling such questions requires calm examination of the patterns you find.

(i)   1 ► 10 = 1+2+3+4+5+6+7+8+9+10 = **55**.

(ii)   Don't painfully calculate the whole thing. It is 1 ► 10 with one more item, 11, added.
1 ► 11 = 55 + 11 = **66**.

(iii)   1 ► 12 = 66 + 12 = **78**.

(iv)   1 ► 13 = 78 + 13 = **91**.

(v)   In (1 ► 200) – (1 ► 199), the 1 ► 200 contains all the numbers in 1 ► 199, plus the number 200. Therefore (1 ► 200) – (1 ► 199) = **200**.

(vi)   Likewise, in (1000 ► 2000) – (1001 ► 1999), by comparison to 1001 ► 1999 the 1000 ► 2000 has an extra 1000 at the beginning and an extra 2000 at the end. Therefore (1000 ► 2000) – (1001 ► 1999) = **3000**.

(vii)   The next question asks you to use algebra to give a more general answer,
$$(a ► b) – ((a+1) ► b) = a + a+1 + a+2 + a+3 + ... + b$$
$$- (\quad a+1 + a+2 + a+3 + ... + b)$$
$$= \quad a$$

(viii) $(1 ► a) + ((a+1) ► b)$ = 1 + 2 + 3 + ... + a   +   a+1 + a+2 + a+3 + ... + b
= 1 ► b

Answer **65**

(i) 321 – 123 = **198**.

(ii) 832 – 238 = **594**.

(iii) Let us call the 3 digits of the first number a, b and c. The subtraction looks like this

	H	T	U
	a	b	c
–	c	b	a

Since c is always smaller than a, we will always need to borrow from the "Tens" column. Before the borrowing, b – b will always be 0, and after the borrowing it will always be 9 with a 1 borrowed from the Hundreds column.

(iv) In principle, a – c is exactly the opposite of c – a, and if they were done as separate arithmetic questions the two results would add up to zero. However they are really *digits* in a single subtraction. When c – a is carried out, it is always negative, so needs borrowing, which adds 10 to the value of c-a, and subtracts 1 from the value of a-c. So the sum of the first and last digits of the subtraction result is zero, plus 10, minus 1 = 9.

Answer 66

(i) Area of vertical faces

First calculate the lengths of the remaining edges, using the edges that are already labelled. This first diagram shows how to do this.

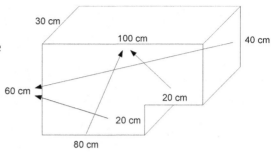

Then calculate the area of each vertical face, as shown below.

The non-rectangular front face can be broken down into two rectangles.

Do not forget the small vertical face that is almost hidden at the bottom of the diagram.

Remember the faces at the back of the diagram.

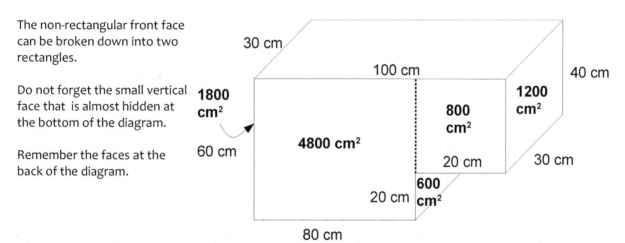

Total area   =   1800 + 2× (4800 + 800) + 600 + 1200
                =   **14800 cm².**

(ii) First find the volume of the tank. The tank is a prism, with cross section shown on the front wall. Area of front wall is 4800+800 = 5600 cm². Distance from front to back = 30 cm. Volume = 5600 × 30 = 168 000 cm³.

Time taken to fill = 168 000 ÷ 100 = 1680 seconds. Minutes = 1680÷60 = 280. Hours =280÷60 = 4 rem 40.

Finishing time = **16:40.**

Answer 67

There are 12 possibilities. The probability is therefore the number of possibilities that meet the requirement (e.g. being even), divided by 12.

The question requires the answer to be in the form of the fraction **in its lowest terms,** so 6/12 is not acceptable; it has to be given as ½.

(i) **1/2.**

(ii) **1/3.**   Beware the trap: "smaller than 5" means 1 to 4, *not* 5.   4/12 = 1/3.

(iii) **1/3.**

(iv) **1/6.**   Again, note that "more than 10" means 11 and 12, *not* 10.   2/12 = 1/6.

(v) **11/12.**

(vi) **2/3.**   1, 10, 11 and 12 contain a "1". 8/12 = 2/3.

(vii) **12.**

(viii) **1/12.**

(ix) **1/36.**   This is because both dice have to show 6. 1/6 × 1/6 = 1/36.

(x) **Thomas.**

Answer 68

On approach is to build up a table of possibilities. You can sketch it out or just imagine it.

Start with the possibilities with the first two throws being 1, but allowing for all possibilities of the **third** throw:

```
111  112  113  114  115  116  117  118
```

Then imagine extending the table downwards to allow for all possibilities of the **second** throw:

```
111  112  113  114  115  116  117  118
121  122  123  124  125  126  127  128
131  132  133  134  135  136  137  138
141  142  143  144  145  146  147  148
151  152  153  154  155  156  157  158
161  162  163  164  165  166  167  168
171  172  173  174  175  176  177  178
181  182  183  184  185  186  187  188
```

You should then be able to imagine another 7 copies of this for the other possibilities for the **first** throw.

```
211  212  213  214  215  216  217  218
221  222  etc  ...  ...  ...  ...  ...
...  ...  ...  ...  ...  ...  ...  ...

311  etc

Tbs continues until the final row
which reads:

881  882  883  884  885  886  887  888
```

(i) **Impossible.** Because the value 9 is not available.

(ii) **Likely.** Because the vast majority of the values are >120.

(iii) **Certain.** If x is any whole number, 4x is even and therefore 4x+8 is even.

(iv) **Unlikely.** For 2x to be <250, x must be <125, which fits only a small proportion of all the possibilities.

(v) **Unlikely.** This requires all three digits to be 7 or 8.

Answer 69

(i)
75 is 5 more than the mean, indicates that the mean is 70.

"The only pair to obtain the same score" indicates that that their score is the most common score, i.e. the mode. **Mode =63**.

(ii)

Philomena scored 6 more than that, i.e. 69.
So far we know the scores are

75	Roberto
69	Philomena
63	Kelvin
63	Calvin
a	Abigail

For the mean to be 70,

$$(75+69+63+63+a) \div 5 = 70$$
=> $(270+a) = 70 \times 5 = 350$
=> $a = 80$

80	Abigail
75	Roberto
69	Philomena
63	Kelvin
63	Calvin

Median = 69.

(iii) **Range = 17.**

(iv) **Abigail's score = 80.**

(v) If Myrtle's score is m,

$$(350 + m) \div 6 = 68$$
$$350 + m = 68 \times 6 = 408$$
$$m = 58 \qquad \text{Myrtle's \textbf{score} = 58}$$

(vi) The scores are: 80, 75, **69, 63,** 63, 58.
Since there is an even number of values, the mean of the middle two (highlighted above) is taken.
Median = 66.

Answer 70

(i)

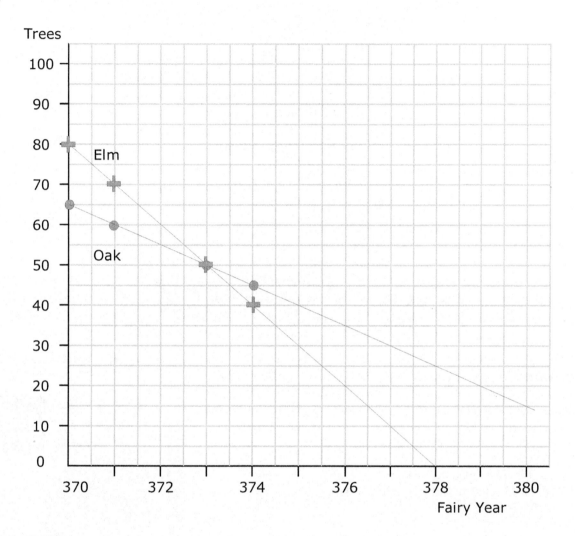

(ii)   379

(iii)   378

(iv)   55.

(v)   60.

Answer 71

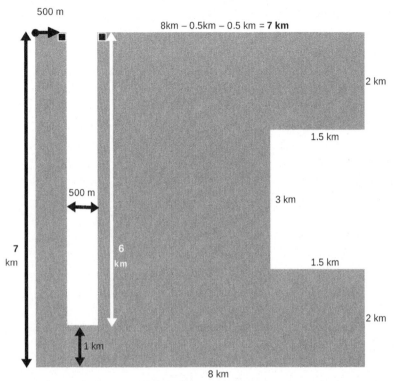

500 m

8km − 0.5km − 0.5 km = **7 km**

2 km

1.5 km

3 km

500 m

1.5 km

7 km

6 km

2 km

1 km

8 km

Tip: Prevent error in perimeter calculations by marking the start point with a blob, and direction with an arrow.
(i) **Perimeter** = 0·5 + 6 + 0·5 + 6 + 7 + 2 + 1·5 + 3 + 1·5 + 2 + 8 + 7 = **45 m**

(ii) **Area**   One standard approach is to break the area into many small rectangular land areas. Here is one such possibility, which produces five rectangles, as shown on the right.

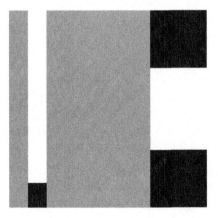

However it is less work to calculate the area of the enclosing rectangle, 7 × 8 = 56 km^2 and then subtract the two sea areas encroaching into the land.

Area = 56 − (0·5×6) − (3×1·5) = 48.**5 km^2**.

(iii) Added area = **3,000,000 m^2**.

(iv) Reduction in perimeter = **12,000 m**

Parallelogram Trap

Imagine a stack of many identical books piled neatly. The side view would be a rectangle. Now imagine the stack pushed a little, with each book sliding (with respect to the book below) a little to the right. The side view would now be approximately a parallelogram.

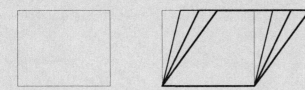 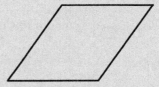

The key observation is that the total area of the side view would have remained the same. So would the width of the **base** and the **height measured perpendicularly to the base**. This is why it is easy to calculate the area of a parallelogram.

Do not fall into the trap of worrying about the length of the diagonal side. The more the book pile leans over, the longer that diagonal side gets, but it makes no difference to the area.

(i) Reduction = **50%**.

Quickest Method. By mentally leaning the walls of the parallelograms (left panel), you can convert each pair of parallelograms into a single rectangle (middle panel) of area 2 × 1·5 m. The triangle of design B fits neatly within that rectangle (right panel). Treating the left side of that figure as the base, the area of the rectangle is base×height, and the area of the triangle is (½) base×height, so the triangle has half the area.

 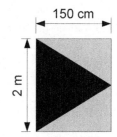

150 cm

2 m

Alternative method. Calculate the area of the two parallelograms together, 2×1·5×1 = 3 m². The area of the triangle is (½)×2×1·5 = 1·5 m². Reduction is therefore 50%.

(ii) Each pattern repeats every 1·5 + 0·5 = 2 m. The total length of the track is 1000 m. Therefore the number of times the pattern is painted is 1000 ÷ 2 = 500. Total area of paint = 500 × 1·5 = 750 m².

Cost = 750 × £80 = **£60,000**.

Answer 73

(i) -27 °C.

(ii) **Yes** it is unusual. **It is lower than all the temperatures in the 2 weeks.**

(iii) There are 6 negative temperatures, 7 positive temperatures and one zero. You can sketch them like this:

- - - - - - 0 + + + + + + +

Therefore, once ranked in order, the median would be the half-way point between the zero and the lowest of the positives (1), which comes to **+0·5°C.**

Answer 74

(i) **9 hours.**

(ii) Tokyo is ahead of London. When it is 06:30 in Tokyo, in London it is 06:30 minus 9 hours. Subtracting this produces a negative number, so it is better to calculate as "06:30 +24:00 – 9:30", i.e.
21:30. Note that this time is on the **previous** day.

(iii) In London time, the flight had started at 09:30 and ended at 21:30. Therefore it had taken **12 hours.**

(iv) 6000 miles in 12 hours is 6000÷12 = **500 miles per hour.**

(v) Duration of play-list = 24×5 min = 120 min = 2 hours
Number of hearings of play-list = duration of flight ÷ duration of play-list = 12/ 2 = **6 times.**

TIME ZONE TRAPS

Plus or minus?

The most common error is to mix up the direction of time differences. One way to prevent this is to visualise a globe or a map and remember that the sun "rises in the east"; indeed that is the reason that Japan, a very easterly country, has a flag that represents its reputation as the land of the rising sun. Imagine the sun starting at the far east (near Japan) and progressively moving west (towards America).

Locations further east see the sun earlier, and therefore experience noon (and any other local times) earlier than locations in the west.

Duration of a journey, given start and end times in different time zones

This can be a journey, or a telephone call. If start and end times are given in different time zones, the safest method is to re-express either the start time into the time zone of the end time, or vice versa. After that a simple subtraction is all you need.

Trap **Double-counting regions of a complex shape**

When you break down an object into parts, be careful not to count any regions of it twice. For example, if you consider the 4 legs of the table to be 4·5 m long, and then add the entire rectangle of the table top, you will have double counted the 4 regions of the table top immediately above the legs.

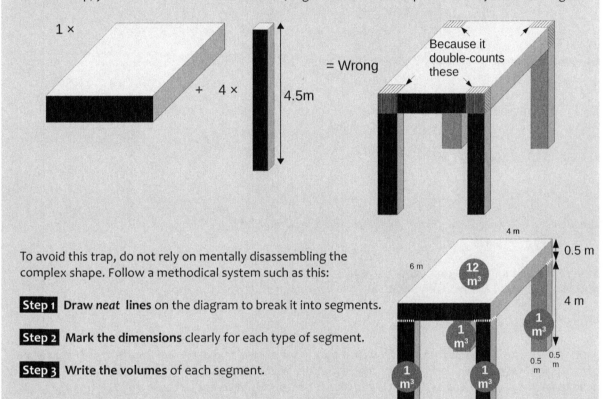

To avoid this trap, do not rely on mentally disassembling the complex shape. Follow a methodical system such as this:

Step 1 Draw *neat* **lines** on the diagram to break it into segments.

Step 2 **Mark the dimensions** clearly for each type of segment.

Step 3 **Write the volumes** of each segment.

(i) Volume of wood = 12 + 4×1 = **16 m³.**

(ii) Do not make the mistake of assuming all four inverted U shapes are the same. The tabletop is rectangular rather than square, so there are two pairs of identical sides. The obvious approach is to calculate the area of the front side (black inverted U) and the right side (grey inverted U) and double their total. However each inverted U is rather intricate so this is prone to error.

An easier approach is to break the shape up in the manner shown for volumes.
Area = Area of top surface + Area of strip running around top surface + Area of legs (excluding top strip)
= 6×4 + 2×(6+4)×0·5 + 4×2×(4×0·5) = 24+10 +16 = **50 m².**

Answer 76

Tip: **Start Small**

In multiplications, additions or subtractions with hidden digits, the hidden value with the lowest place values is often the best place to start. This is because it cannot be affected by "carrying" from the other hidden values.

(i) $518 - 3\square 2 = 19\square$

The lowest place value is the **Units column**. This reads 8-2 = $\square$, so $\square$ must be 6. So the equation now reads:
        $518 - 3\square 2 = 196$

The lowest remaining place value is now the Tens column. This reads $1 - \square = 9$. This works only for $\square$ being 2, with 1 being borrowed from the Hundreds column.

Answer: **518 – 322 = 196**

(ii) $98\square - \square\square 2 = 473$

The lowest place value is the Units: $\square$-2=3, therefore that $\square$ must be 5, i.e.
        $985 - \square\square 2 = 473$

At this stage, although you can follow the above steps for the remaining two digit, it might be easier to just calculate 985 – 473, which comes to 512. This allows you to write down the answer:

Answer: **985 – 512 = 473**

(iii) Here there is a hidden value in the Units position, in the second number. We know that the **Units column** of the multiplication must read $3 \times \square = 7$. Think about the last digits of the 3 times table (from 0×3 to 9×3; no need to go to 10 and beyond as the last digits repeat themselves of course). They are <u>0</u> <u>3</u> <u>6</u> <u>9</u> 12 15 1<u>8</u> 21 2<u>4</u> 2<u>7</u>. Only 3×9 gives a final digit of 7. So now we can write
        $2\,\square 3 \quad \times \quad 9 \quad = \quad \square\square 17$

Now we know that the Units column will provide a 2 to be carried over to the Tens. The **Tens column** therefore reads: $\square \times 9 \; +2$ (the carry) = 1. With this formula it looks like the last digit of $\square \times 9$ is 1-2 = -1. Think what happens in arithmetic **within a particular column** if you start with 1 and subtract 2: you get not -1 but 9 (and a borrow from the next, higher value, column). So $\square \times 9 = 9$, i.e. $\square = 1$.
        $2\,1\,3 \quad \times \quad 9 \quad = \quad \square\square 17$
Then multiply 213 by 9 to fill in the remaining two $\square$s.
Answer: $2\,1\,3 \quad \times \quad 9 \quad = \quad 191\,7$

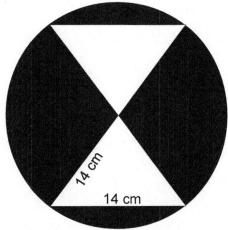

(i) Two sets of 3 sides, each of 14 cm.

Total = 2 × 3 × 14 = **84 cm**.

(ii) Area = πr^2

$= (22/7) \times 14 \times 14$

$= 44 \times 14$

$= 616 \text{ cm}^2$.

(iii) He can arrange them as shown below. The angle at the top of an equilateral triangle is 60 degrees. Therefore the number that can be arranged to form this shape = 360 ÷ 60 = **6**.

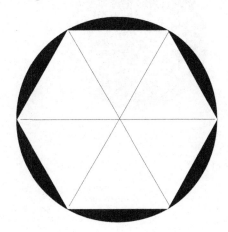

Answer 78

Any question of this type is asking for the ratio of areas.

Step 1. Decide which unit, cm or m, you are going to use for your working. If almost all the measurements are in one unit, it is usually easiest to convert the others to that unit. Here there is one piece of information in each unit, so just pick either cm or m.

Step 2. Calculate the area of all the lilies.
The area of a single lily can be calculated as shown below.

0.1 m

$$A = \pi r^2$$
$$= 3.14 \times 0.1^2$$
$$= 0.0314 m^2$$

The total area of all 50 lilies is $50 \times 0.0314 = 1.57 m^2$.

Step 3. Calculate the area of the pond
$$= 1.57 \times 10$$
$$= 15.7 \ m^2$$

Step 4. Probability of hitting a lily = area of lilies ÷ area of pond
$$= 1.57 / 15.7$$
$$= \mathbf{1/10}$$ \qquad\qquad (Or you can give it as 0·1)

Answer 79   This question is very easy unless you stumble into the infamous fencepost trap

Trap: **Fencepost problem in page ranges**

This type of question is extremely simple but many are caught out by the fencepost problem. If you were caught out, ask yourself these questions (see bottom of page for answers).

Step 1.
　　　What is 3 minus 1?　　　Answer _____
　　　A book chapter running from page 1 to page 3 is how many pages long? _____ pages

Step 2
　　　What is 5 minus 1?　　　Answer _____
　　　A book chapter running from page 1 to page 5 is how many pages long? _____ pages

Step 3
　　　Why is the number of pages always one more than the result of the subtraction?

　　　Answer _____

　　　_____

Step 4
　　　What is 5 minus 4?　　　Answer _____
　　　A book chapter running from page 4 to page 5 is how many pages long? _____ pages

Step 5
　　　A book chapter running from page x to page y is how many pages long?
　　　(Give the answer as a formula in terms of x and y)　　　Answer _____

(i) In pages 18 to 57 the number of pages is 57-18+1 = 58-18=40.
In pages 23 to 52 the number of pages is 52-23+1 = 53-23 = 30
Reduction = 40-30 =10
Reduction as a percentage = 10/40 = **25%**.

(ii) Pages read in 60 minutes = 2×15=30. However, the fencepost error is to give the answer as 60+30. In fact, at the start of the period, she was just about to start page 60; therefore at the end she is just about to start page 90. That means the page she has just read is **page 89**.

Answers to Infobox questions
[1] 2. 3. [2] 4. 5. [3] Because both the first and last are counted. [4] 1. 2. [5] y-x+1.

Answer 80

Such questions can be solved with algebra but before resorting to this, try to see if there are any pieces of information that can immediately allow you to fill in parts of the table.

The third sentence is exactly that, as it directly gives you usable information. You can start filling in the table like this:

	Harry	Ron
Orange	?	?
Apple	2	4
Pear	?	?

With this, you can then apply the 4th sentence (Ron, equal apple and orange) fills in one more blank, and then the 1st sentence (Orange: Harry 5 more than Ron)

	Harry	Ron
Orange	9	4
Apple	2	4
Pear	?	?

The final sentence (Harry orange = Ron pear) then reveals Ron pear, and the 2nd sentence gives Harry pear.

	Harry	Ron
Orange	9	4
Apple	2	4
Pear	6	9

Answer 81

Converting between perimeters and areas is a common need in examination questions. Remember that for a square, the perimeter is 4 times one side, and the area is the square of the side.

(i)
Perimeter =480 m. Side = 480÷4 = 120 m
Area = 120 × 120 = 14400 m^2.
Time taken if done by one person = 14400 min
Time taken if done by 20 people = 14400÷20 = 1440÷2 = **720 minutes**

(ii)
Time taken if done by one person = 480/1 = 480 min
Time taken if done by 20 people = 480/20 = **24 minutes**

(iii)
Extra time taken = 480 – 14 = 456 minutes.
456 ÷ 60 = 7 remainder 36
Extra time taken = **7 hours 36 minutes.**

Tip: **Discount devastation**

Have a clear method for the 3 types of discount question.

A Prior price and final price stated, what is the discount percentage?
Reduction in price divided by prior price: express this as a percentage

B. Prior price and discount percentage stated, what is the final price?
Either:

Calculate the change in price as   (discount percentage ÷ 100)×price
Then subtract it from the prior price.
    e.g. £50 beforehand, 20% discount. Change in price =20/100×50=1000/100=£10.
    final price = 50-10 = £40.

Or:

Calculate the percentage of the price remaining as 100-discount percentage.
Then multiply by the prior price.
    e.g. £50 beforehand, 20% discount. Final price = 80/100×50=4000/100=£40.

C. **Final** price and discount percentage stated, what is the prior price? `Many pupils find this difficult`

The key is to multiply by 100/(100-percentage), not simply add that percentage.
This is because the percentage described was of the prior price, not the final price.
e.g. £45 after a 10% discount. **DO NOT** add 10% to £45 to give the answer £4·95: this is wrong.
Instead the correct method is to calculate 45×100/(100-10)=45×100/90=45×10/9=5×10=**£50**.

(i) Pre-sale price = £21×100/(100-30) = 21×10/7 = 3×10 = **£30**.
        You can check this by calculating 30% off £30: it is £9, giving £21.

(ii) Pre-sale price = 2×£25 = £50. Money he has = £40. Shortfall=50-40=£10.
Percentage reduction required = 10/50=1/5= **20%**.
        Note that the denominator must be the prior price. Discounts are always described as a proportion of the prior price, not of
        the final price.

(iii) Price before Zanzibar Express card surcharge = £40 – 30%of £40 = 70% of £40 = 70×40/100=7×4=£28.
Zanzibar Express card surcharge = 5% of £28=5/100×28=140/100=£1·40.
        Note: the Zanzibar Express card surcharge is on the discounted price, not the original price.
Price paid by Ivan = 28+1·40 = **£29·40**.

Answer 83

(i)   This can be answered without calculating the areas themselves.

The flag could be cut in two, with the black triangle's right-hand tip touching the dividing line.

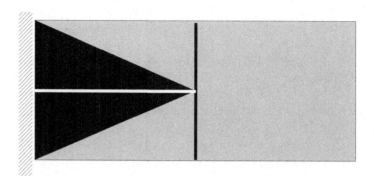

The triangle has half the area of the left-hand rectangle.
If this does not appear obvious, try drawing a horizontal line through the triangle to meet the right-hand tip. Now the left side of the flag is made up of an upper and lower half. In each half, the black area is obviously equal to the grey area, i.e. is half the area.

The black area therefore is ¼ the area of the whole flag.

Percentage = **25%**.

(ii)   The 25% is ¼ not 1/3, but is still correct. The black area is ¼ *of the whole flag*, but as a proportion *of the grey area* it is (1/4)÷(3/4)=1/3.

The flagmaster-general replied that "we have indeed done this correctly: the black area is one third of the grey area."

(iii)   Again it is not essential to calculate the actual areas. Each black triangle can be considered to sit inside a rectangle that is 1/4 the area of the flag. Each black triangle is half the area of that rectangle, and therefore 1/8 of the area of the flag.

Percentage needing to change colour = **0%**.

Answer 84

Method

This type of question is asking you to rapidly compare many probabilities. It is best to calculate the probabilities and write them down, to save having to calculate any of them more than once.

Step 1. Calculate the total number of possibilities in each barrel.

Step 2. Calculate the probabilities of each possibility, by dividing the number of possibilities by the total.

Short-cut note. For problems of identifying the largest or smallest of a set of numbers, answers that turn out to have many decimal places do not always have to be calculated to very many places. Just make sure you note to yourself (for example, with the "..." symbol) that the answer has more digits.

Barrel	I	II	III	IV	V	VI
Helicopter	2	1	4	3	5	6
Video game	2	3	2	1	2	8
Springs	3	4	2	1	3	10
Total	7	8	8	5	10	24
Helicopter	0·28...	0·125	0·5	0·6	0·5	0·25
Video game	0·28...	0·375	0·25	0·2	0·2	0·333...
Springs	0·42...	0·5	0·25	0·2	0·3	0·41...

(i) Barrel **IV**.

(ii) Barrel **II**.

(iii) **1/3**.

8 possibilities out of 24 = 8÷24 = 1/3. The question specifically asks for a fraction in its lowest terms, so 8/24 is not accepted.

(iv) Total Helicopters = 2+1+4+3+5+6=21
Helicopters dropped = 1+6=7. Helicopters escaped with 21-7=14. Proportion escaped with = 14/21 = **2/3**.

Answer 85

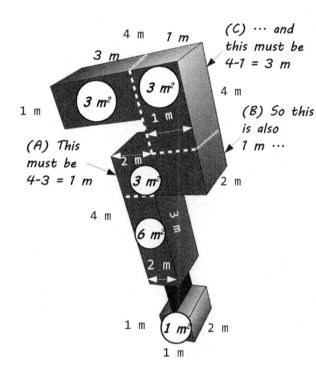

4 m   1 m

3 m

3 m²

3 m²

1 m

1 m

(A) This
must be
4-3 = 1 m

2 m

3 m²

4 m

3 m

6 m²

2 m

(C) ··· and
this must be
4-1 = 3 m

4 m

(B) So this
is also
1 m ···

2 m

1 m   1 m²   2 m

1 m

Method

Step 1 Break the object into cuboids (neat rectangular blocks). In this diagram this has been done with dotted lines.

Step 2 Label the unlabelled edge lengths. Remember that some edges of the whole object must now be broken into two parts.

In some cases you must use additional or subtraction to calculate these. In this case, notice the three stages required (A) to (C).

Step 3 Mark the areas on the front face. Don't worry about the volumes for now.

Step 4 Calculate the total volume as the total front face area multiplied by the depth (2m in this case).

Alternatively you can calculate the volume for each cuboid in turn, but it would be more calculation and therefore more chance of error.

(i) (3+3+3+6) × 2 = 16 × 2 = **32 m³**.

(ii) (3+3+3+6) = **15 m²**.

(iii) These walls run from the perimeter of the front surface to the perimeter of the back surface. Can you imagine them lifted off the surface of the object as a strip? How long and how wide would the strip be? It would be a loop of length equal to the perimeter of the front surface, and width 2m. The perimeter is 4 + 4+1+3+2+4+2+1+3+1 = 25 m. The area is therefore 25 × 2= **50 m²**.

(iv) Yellow stripes are painted in 3 places:

> *front* and
> *back*, where they are 25 m each
> *front-to-back*, which occurs at every corner on the front face: 10 places × 2 m = 20 m.

Total = 25 + 25 + 20 = **70 m**.

Answer 86

Notice that if you add up the 3 equations, you have all 3 cats present twice. This means the total is 2 × the total of all 3 cats. Therefore you can work out what the total of all 3 cats is; by subtracting any pair you get the third.

$$P + Q = 9$$
$$Q + R = 11$$
$$R + P = 14$$

Sum:

$$2(P+Q+R) = 34$$
$$P+Q+R = 17$$

From this, subtract each of the first 3 equations in turn (one by one), obtaining:

$$P = 6 \text{ kg}$$
$$Q = 3 \text{ kg}$$
$$R = 8 \text{ kg}$$

Do a final check with the numbers you obtain to make sure they match the question:

6+3=9,
3+8=11,
8+6=14

(ii) Quick method

If the scales have been over-reading by 1 kg, and each reading was with two cats, then you should be able to adjust for the error by removing 0·5kg from each cat. So let's try the following:

$$P = 5 \cdot 5 \text{ kg}$$
$$Q = 2 \cdot 5 \text{ kg}$$
$$R = 7 \cdot 5 \text{ kg}$$

Checking against the question, these answers fit the 3 totals printed, minus 1.

Slow method.

Write out the correct totals, i.e. removing one kg from each total of two cats

$$P + Q = 8$$
$$Q + R = 10$$
$$R + P = 13$$

Then proceed as above, and you will reach the same answer as the quick method.

Answer 87

The question is made of very simple components, but you must navigate the fencepost problem, *twice*.

(i) Number of gaps between stairs = 3 m ÷ 0·2 m = 15. However, this is *not* the number of stairs he steps on, because of the fencepost problem.

Fencepost problem

|___| 2 fenceposts, 1 gap between them

|___|___| 3 fenceposts, 2 gap between them

|___|___|___| 4 fenceposts, 3 gap between them

The number of stairs stepped on is 15+1 = **16.**

(ii) Number of *gaps between* stairs = (51-1)×15 = 750.

Number of stairs ***stepped on*** = 750+1 = **751.**

(iii) Angle turned through for each stair = 360 degrees ÷ 36 = 10 degrees

Number of circles turned through = 750÷10 = **75.**

Answer **88**

Although these questions can in principle be solved without it, they are most easily solved with algebra.

Symbols for ages *now:*

Colin   = n
Cerys   = s
Charlie = e

Using these symbols, the question tells us:

$n+1 = 2[(s+1)+(e+1)]$ Equation [1]
$s = e + 4$ Equation [2]
$n = 3 (s+1)$ Equation [3]

Use [3] to remove n from [1]

$3(s+1) +1 = 2 s + 2 + 2 e+2$
$3 s + 4 = 2 s + 2 e + 4$
$s = 2 e$

Use [2] to remove s from what remains

$e + 4 = 2 e$
$4 = e$ Age of Charlie = **4 years**

Using the same two equations in reverse order,
By [2]
$s = 8$
By [3]
$n = 27$

(ii) In y years, Colin will be 27+y, and Charlie will be 4+y

$27 + y = 2 (4+y)$
$27 + y = 8 + 2y$
$19 = y$

Year = 1990 + 19 = **2009.**

Answer 89

(i) to (iv):

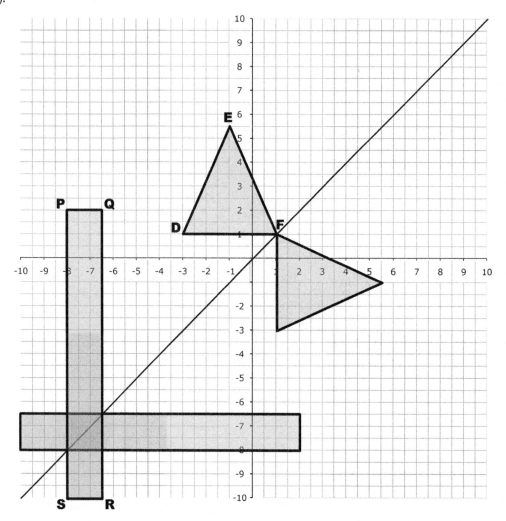

(v) The overlap is a square of side 1·5.
Area of overlap = 1·5 × 1·5 = 2·25 = **2 ¼**.

Answer 90

Tip: **Ratios**

If you are given a ratio of counts of items (or people) in different categories, and a total count, and asked to calculate how many of each category there are, imagine the ratio values to be describing the front row of an "army" of items advancing towards you.

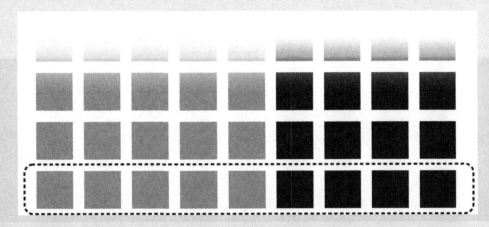

Step 1 Consider the ratio to describes the items (or people) in the front row (dotted line in the example sketch above). Here, there are 5 girls (grey) and 4 boys (black).

Calculate the total number items in the front row. Here it is 9.

Step 2 Therefore how many rows are there? Here it is 90 ÷ 9 = 10 rows.

Step 3 Therefore how many people of each category? In 10 rows (of 5 girls + 4 boys) there would be 50 girls + 40 boys.

(i)
Number of girls = 90/9 × 5 = 50. Number of boys = 90/9 × 4 = 40. Excess number of girls = 50-40 = **10**.

(ii)
Rows = 90÷(1+2)=90/3=30. Number with spectacles = 30×1 = **30**.

(iii)
Rows = 90÷(1+8)=90/9=10. Number who can sing = 8×10 = **80**.

Printed in Great Britain
by Amazon

46639215R00037